Flying Squirrel at Acorn Place

To Billy, A.J., and Hannah. — B.G.W.

To S^2 with love. — K^2

Illustrations copyright © 1998 Kristin Kest
Book copyright © 1998 Trudy Corporation, 353 Main Avenue, Norwalk, CT 06851,
and the Smithsonian Institution, Washington, DC 20560.

Soundprints is a division of Trudy Corporation, Norwalk, Connecticut.

Book layout: Diane Hinze Kanzler

First Edition 1998
10 9 8 7 6 5 4 3 2 1
Printed in Singapore

Acknowledgements:
   Our very special thanks to Dr. Charles Handley of the Department of Vertebrate Zoology
at the Smithsonian Institution's National Museum of Natural History for his curatorial review.

Library of Congress Cataloging-in-Publication Data

Winkelman, Barbara Gaines 1961–

Flying Squirrel at Acorn Place / written by Barbara Gaines Winkelman; illustrated by Kristin Kest.
          p.   cm.
Summary: Flying Squirrel is awakened by a giant paw poking into his rooftop nest and decides it is time
to look for a new home.
          ISBN 1-56899-669-1
1. Flying Squirrels—Juvenile fiction. [1. Flying Squirrels—Fiction. 2. Squirrels—Fiction.]
I. Kest, Kristin, ill.   II. Title.
          PZ10.3.W6847F1 1998   98-6047
          [E]—dc21   CIP
                                                                                     AC

Flying Squirrel at Acorn Place

by Barbara Gaines Winkelman

Illustrated by Kristin Kest

Soundprints™
Where Children Discover...

Flying Squirrel lives under a broken shingle on the roof of the stone house at Acorn Place. Early one morning, he wakes with a start to see a large paw coming toward him. Flying Squirrel presses himself far back in his nest, barely escaping the long, sharp nails of a house cat.

Outside, a blue jay begins to call. "Jay! Jay! Jay!" the bird scolds. The cat has come much too close to the blue jay's nest. The cat darts from the roof to the safety of the house, forgetting about Flying Squirrel—for now.

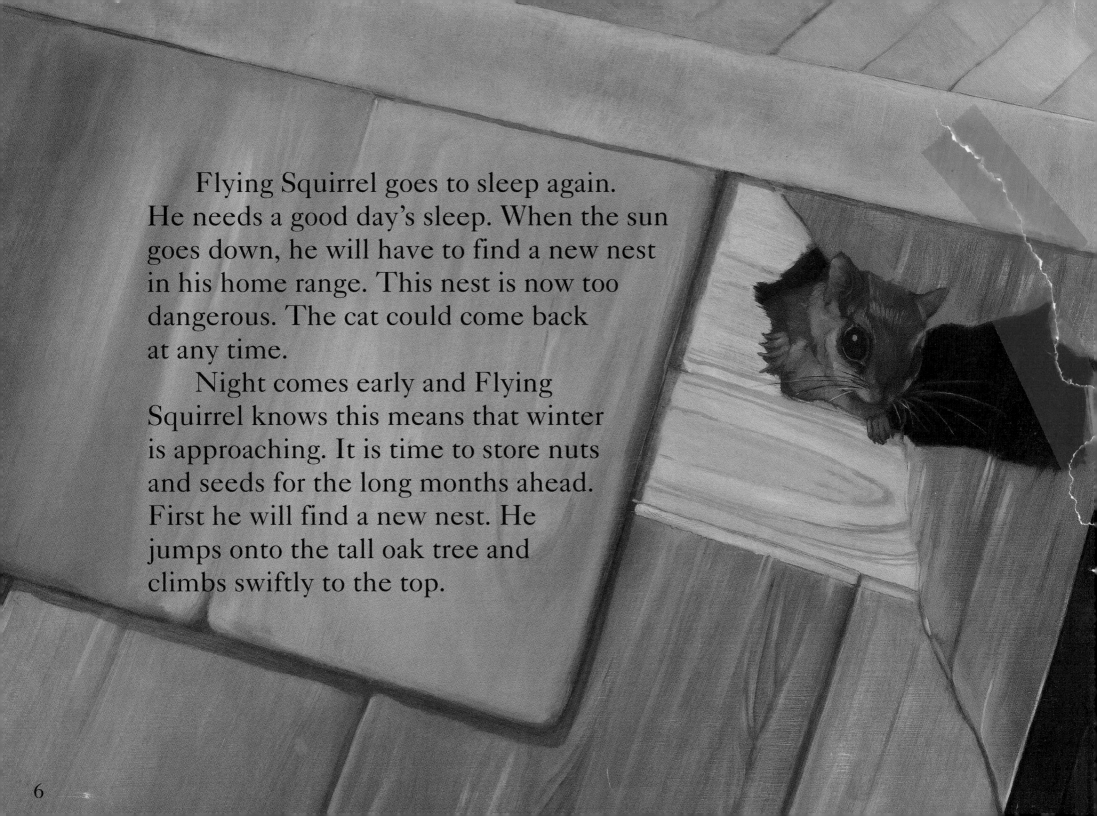

Flying Squirrel goes to sleep again. He needs a good day's sleep. When the sun goes down, he will have to find a new nest in his home range. This nest is now too dangerous. The cat could come back at any time.

Night comes early and Flying Squirrel knows this means that winter is approaching. It is time to store nuts and seeds for the long months ahead. First he will find a new nest. He jumps onto the tall oak tree and climbs swiftly to the top.

Flying Squirrel leaps from the tree into the night. He holds his small feet in tight to gain speed, then he stretches all four legs out wide. The loose, furry flap of skin—or patagium—opens like a sail and he soars over the backyard.

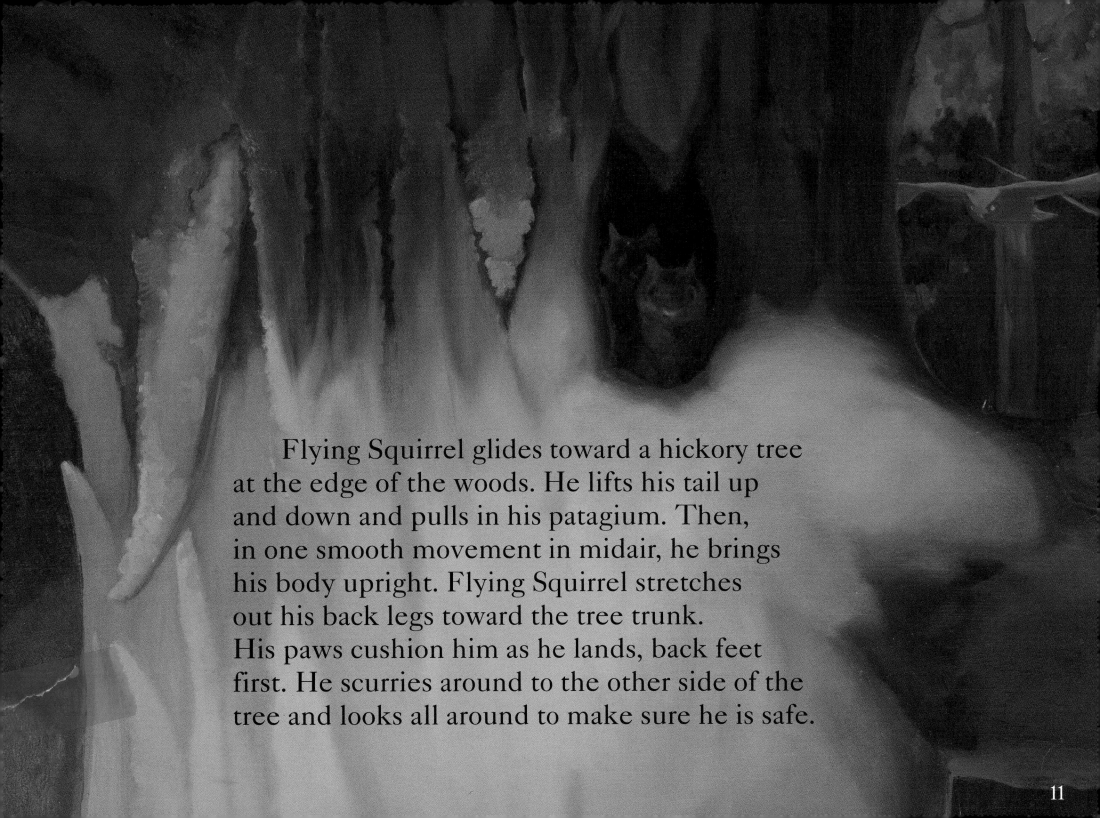

Flying Squirrel glides toward a hickory tree
at the edge of the woods. He lifts his tail up
and down and pulls in his patagium. Then,
in one smooth movement in midair, he brings
his body upright. Flying Squirrel stretches
out his back legs toward the tree trunk.
His paws cushion him as he lands, back feet
first. He scurries around to the other side of the
tree and looks all around to make sure he is safe.

"Tsepp, tsepp, tsepp!" Other flying squirrels are warning him that danger is near. Flying Squirrel looks up quickly and sees the yellow eyes and tufts of feathers of the great horned owl. The fierce hunter is flying straight at him.

Flying Squirrel dives into a hole in the tree. Inside, there are two other flying squirrels in the nest. The three roll over and over, each trying to be at the bottom of the nest, hidden from the outside. They wait for the owl to go away.

Flying Squirrel cannot tell if the owl has gone. Soft feathers on her wings and feet muffle the owl's movements, making her wingbeats soundless.

The owl lives in the middle of Flying Squirrel's home range. No matter where Flying Squirrel is, he knows a good hiding place to escape from danger. He has explored every hole, crack, and crevice of this area.

After a long wait inside the tree, Flying Squirrel peeks from his hiding place. The owl is nowhere to be seen. It is safe for Flying Squirrel to continue his journey.

Flying Squirrel climbs to a high branch
and pushes off. He sails without a sound from tree
to tree. By tilting his patagium left or right, he steers
in graceful curves around branches in his path.

After each glide, he climbs up the nearest tree,
and takes off once again. When he lands on a black
oak tree with an old woodpecker hole, he stops.
This is where he will make his new sleeping nest.

Flying Squirrel busily pads the woodpecker hole with pieces of bark. On the ground underneath the tree, he finds a dried grapevine. He shreds some of it up and puts the wispy fibers on top of the bark. The nest is now comfortable and warm enough for sleeping. This is only one of Flying Squirrel's nests throughout his home range. He has a special use for each.

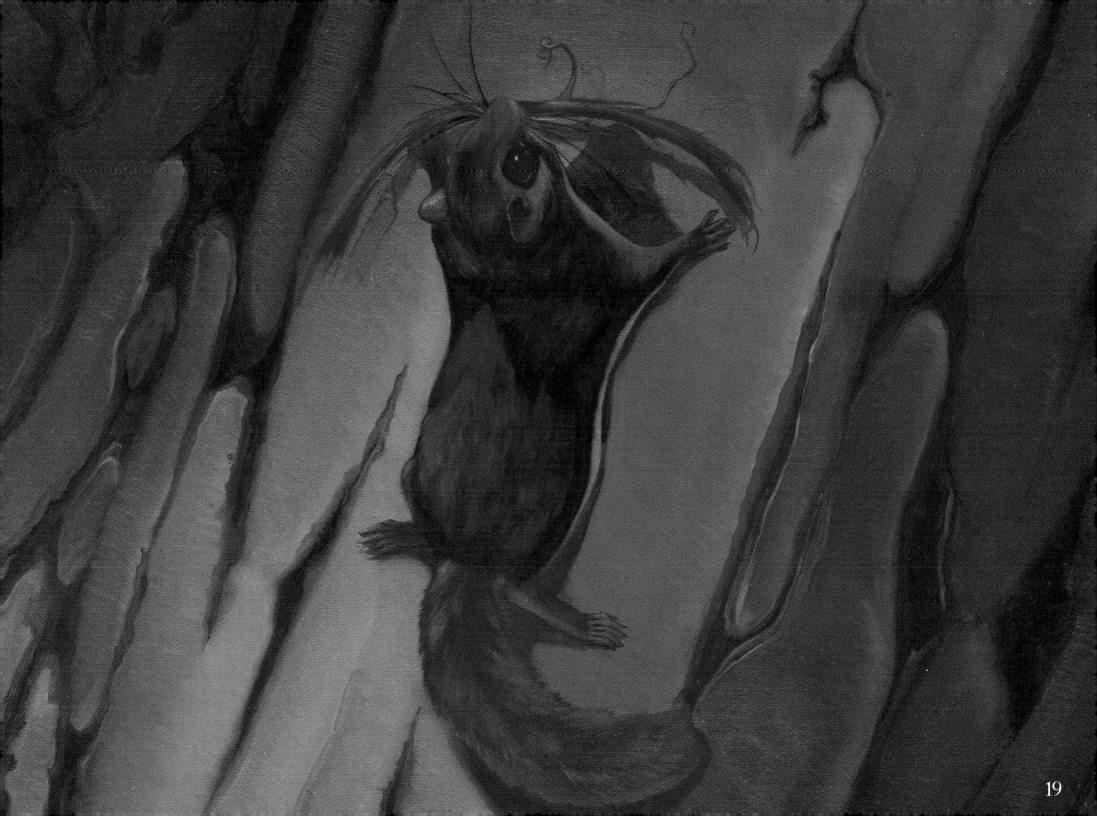

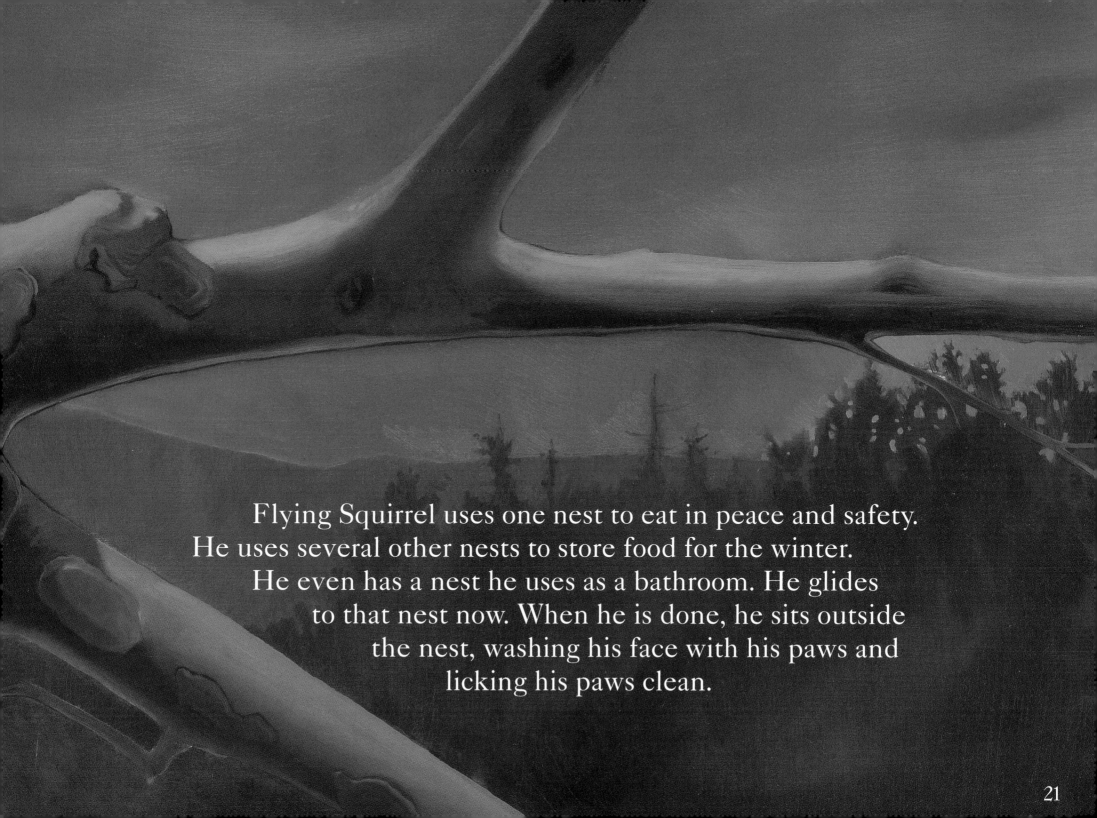

Flying Squirrel uses one nest to eat in peace and safety.
He uses several other nests to store food for the winter.
He even has a nest he uses as a bathroom. He glides
to that nest now. When he is done, he sits outside
the nest, washing his face with his paws and
licking his paws clean.

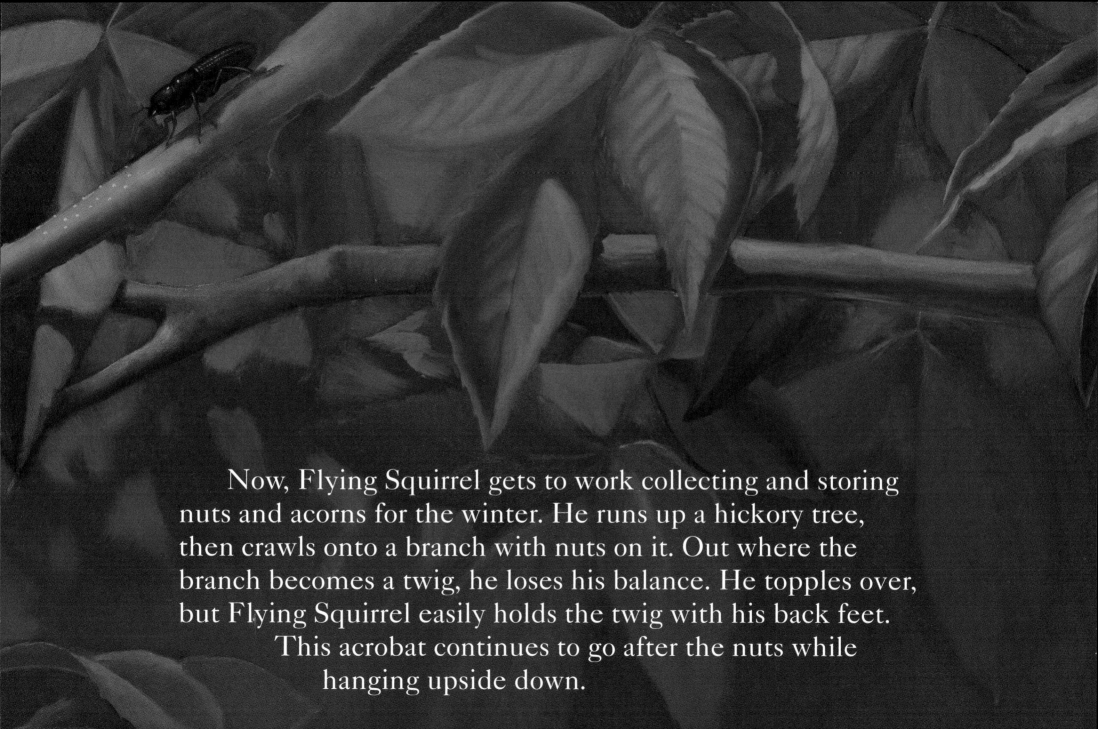

Now, Flying Squirrel gets to work collecting and storing nuts and acorns for the winter. He runs up a hickory tree, then crawls onto a branch with nuts on it. Out where the branch becomes a twig, he loses his balance. He topples over, but Flying Squirrel easily holds the twig with his back feet. This acrobat continues to go after the nuts while hanging upside down.

Flying Squirrel reaches for a hickory nut at the end
of the twig. Still clinging with his back feet, he picks the nut
off the tree with his front feet. He chews off the nut's husk,
and lets the husk fall to the ground.

Holding the nut in his forepaws, Flying Squirrel uses
his lower incisors—his long, front teeth—to cut notches
on either side of the base of the nut. These notches are like
handles, and make it easier for him to carry the nut.

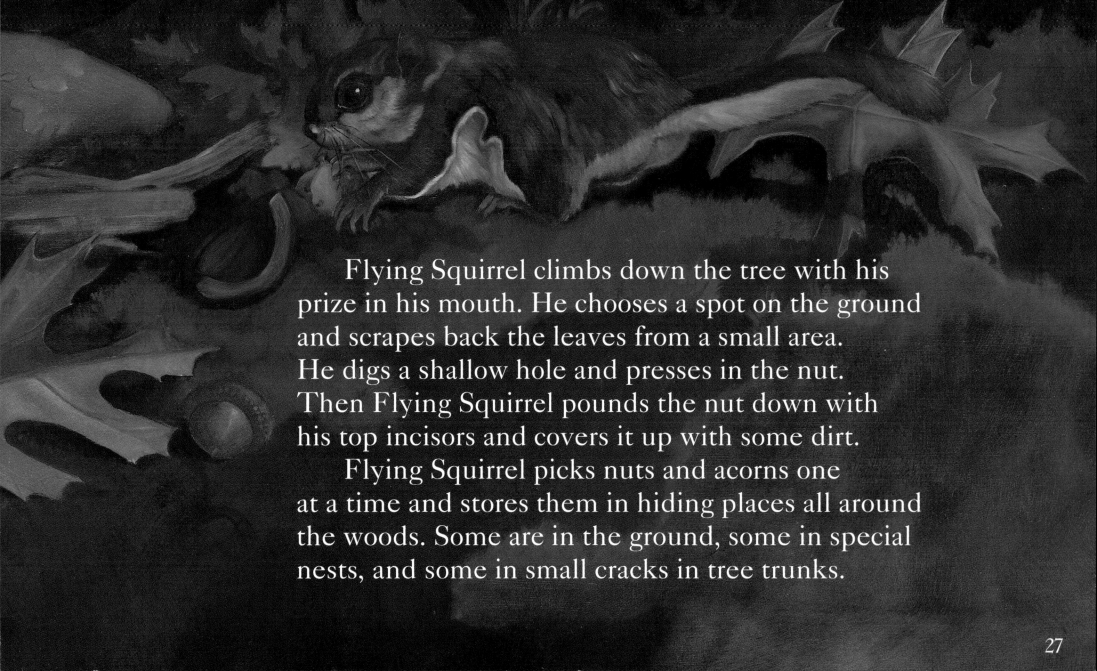

Flying Squirrel climbs down the tree with his prize in his mouth. He chooses a spot on the ground and scrapes back the leaves from a small area. He digs a shallow hole and presses in the nut. Then Flying Squirrel pounds the nut down with his top incisors and covers it up with some dirt.

Flying Squirrel picks nuts and acorns one at a time and stores them in hiding places all around the woods. Some are in the ground, some in special nests, and some in small cracks in tree trunks.

After a few hours, Flying Squirrel is very hungry. Instead of eating any of the nuts he's stored for winter, he glides back to the stone house, where there is an unending source of food—the birdfeeder.

Reaching the backyard, Flying Squirrel pulls in his patagium, lifts his tail, and drifts down in a spiraling pattern. He makes a gentle, four-footed landing on top of the birdfeeder. Scrambling to the tray, he finds the other flying squirrels from the hole in the hickory tree. They all sit together, eating sunflower seeds.

The sky is becoming lighter—
dawn is breaking. It has been a busy
night and Flying Squirrel is tired.
He runs up a tree and glides off to
his new nest in the black oak tree.

When snow covers the ground in the winter
ahead, he will make other trips to the birdfeeder.
If he gets too cold, he'll swoop over to cuddle
with the flying squirrels in the hickory tree.
But for now, he sleeps—safely tucked away
from cats and owls—in the woods behind
the stone house at Acorn Place.

About the Flying Squirrel

Southern flying squirrels are found in the eastern half of the United States and along the coast, from Canada down to east Texas, Mexico, and Honduras. They grow to between eight and ten inches in length, and weigh two to four ounces.

Flying squirrels do not really fly; they glide from a high point to a lower point. Most glides are from 20 to 60 feet, but there is a record of a flying squirrel gliding 300 feet.

Flying squirrels eat nuts, berries, seeds, insects, sap, lichens, and meat. They nest in holes in trees, in attics or the roofs of houses, in birdhouses, and sometimes in abandoned crow or hawk nests.

Flying squirrels are nocturnal creatures—they stay awake at night and sleep during the day. Their large black eyes help them see in the dark. For communication, they make high-pitched chirps and squeaks. Some of these sounds are so high they cannot be heard by the human ear, but can awaken a sleeping dog.

In winter, flying squirrels nest in groups to stay warm. When it gets extremely cold they go into a torpor—their bodies slow down to a deep sleep-like state. They can stay in this state for days, sometimes weeks.

Glossary

fibers: Fine threads of plants or other materials.

home range: The area a flying squirrel lives in and uses for all its activity. It can be up to five acres.

husk: The outer covering or jacket of some nuts, seeds, or fruit.

incisors: Long, strong, upper and lower front teeth.

patagium: Folds of loose, furry skin along the sides of the flying squirrel's body that stretch out between the front and back feet like sails or a parachute when the flying squirrel glides.

Points of Interest in this Book

pp. 10-11: two flying squirrels hiding in tree.

pp. 12-13: lichen on shagbark hickory tree.

pp. 20-21: sycamore or plane tree.

pp. 22-23: bark-gnawing beetle, hickory nut husks.

pp. 24-25: tiger moth.

pp. 26-27: northern red salamander.